FORENSIC SCIENCE INVESTIGATED

SOLVING HISTORY'S | MYSTERIES

WRITTEN BY:
Rebecca Stefoff

Marshall Cavendish
Benchmark
New York

MARSHALL CAVENDISH BENCHMARK
99 WHITE PLAINS ROAD
TARRYTOWN, NEW YORK 10591-5502
www.marshallcavendish.us

LIBRARY OF CONGRESS CATALOGING-IN-PUBLICATION DATA
Stefoff, Rebecca, 1951-
Solving history's mysteries / by Rebecca Stefoff.
p. cm. — (Forensic science investigated)
Includes bibliographical references and index.
ISBN 978-0-7614-3081-0
1. Forensic sciences—History—Case studies—Juvenile literature.
2. Criminal investigation—History—Case studies—Juvenile literature.
I. Title.
HV8073.S7326 2009
363.2509—dc22
2008003628

EDITOR: Christina Gardeski   PUBLISHER: Michelle Bisson
ART DIRECTOR: Anahid Hamparian   SERIES DESIGNER: Kristen Branch

Photo Research by Anne Burns Images

Cover Photo by *Corbis*/Supreme Council for Antiquities/Handout/Reuters
Back Cover Photo by *Phototake*/Terry Why

The photographs in this book are used with permission and through the courtesy of:
iStockphoto: pp. 1, 3 (hand Chris Hutchinson, cells David Marchal). *Corbis*: p. 4 Mike
Nelson/epa; p. 10 Andre Ficte/zefa; p. 14 Todd Gipstein; p. 19 Gianni Dagli; p. 22
Underwood & Underwood; p. 26 Supreme Council of Antiquities/epa; p. 27 Egyptian
Antiquity Department/Handout/Reuters; p. 34 Vincent Kessler/Reuters; p. 38
Hulton-Deutsch Collection; p. 45 Butsenko Anton/ITAR-TASS; p. 48 Layne Kennedy;
p. 51 Bettman; p. 53 Corbis; p. 57 Smithsonian Institute; pp. 59, 61 Pilar Olivares/Reuters;
p. 63 Visuals Unlimited; p. 66 Christophe Boisvieux; p. 78 Ian Harwood/Ecoscene.
SuperStock: pp. 7, 28. *Alamy Images*: pp. 30, 39 Mary Evans Picture Library; p. 72 GC
Minerals; p. 83 Robert Harding Picture Library. *Beinecke Rare Book and Manuscript
Library*: p. 69.

Printed in Malaysia
1 3 5 6 4 2

Cover: Egyptian, French, and American scientists and artists used forensic techniques
to create an image of the ancient king Tutankhamen

CONTENTS

The discovery of Tutankhamen's tomb raised questions about the king's life—and his death. Modern forensic science has answered some of those questions.

WHAT IS FORENSICS?

A KING DIED 3,300 years ago and was laid to rest in Egypt's royal burial ground, the Valley of the Kings. When his tomb was discovered in 1922, the world was fascinated with the young pharaoh Tutankhamen and his extraordinary treasures. No one, however, knew how he died. Some modern investigators have suggested that Tutankhamen was murdered—and have even named a suspect.

For years the people of northern Europe have found strange human bodies with leathery skin in peat bogs, wet deposits of vegetation that people harvest to burn as fuel. These "bog people" are men, women, and children wearing the clothes and jewelry of hundreds, even thousands, of years ago. Many of them bear gruesome evidence of torture. Who were they, and why did they end up in the bogs?

Napoleon Bonaparte was the most feared man in Europe in the early nineteenth century. He conquered half the continent and made himself emperor of France before the British defeated him and shipped him off to exile on a remote island. There he died in 1821 in agonizing pain. Ever since then people have wondered: Was Napoleon poisoned? Some have turned to modern science for the answer to that question.

In the long, tragic history of war between the U.S. Army and American Indians, one of the bloodiest dates is June 25, 1876. On that day, more than two hundred men under the command of Lieutenant Colonel George Armstrong Custer clashed with American Indian warriors—and lost. "Custer's Last Stand," as the battle was called, became the subject of legends and tales. Yet since the 1980s, researchers at the battle site have learned much about what really happened on that fateful day.

Our knowledge of the past is full of holes. Today, however, historical researchers are taking a new look at many old mysteries and unanswered questions. They are improving our understanding of the past through **forensic science**, which is the use of scientific methods and tools to investigate crimes.

▲ Napoleon Bonaparte, self-crowned emperor of France, is another monarch who, according to some theories, died under suspicious circumstances.

The term "forensic" comes from ancient Rome, where people debated matters of law in a public meeting place called the Forum. The Latin word *forum* gave rise to *forensic,* meaning "relating to courts of law or to public debate." Today "forensics" has several meanings. One is the art of speaking in debates, which is why some schools have forensics clubs or teams for students who want to learn debating skills. The best-known meaning of "forensics," though, is crime solving through forensic science.

Fascination with forensics explains the popularity of many recent TV shows, movies, and books, but crime and science have been linked for a long time. The first science used in criminal investigation was medicine, and one of the earliest reports of forensic medicine comes from ancient Rome. In 44 BCE, the Roman leader Julius Caesar was stabbed to death not far from the Forum. A physician named Antistius examined the body and found that Caesar had received twenty-three stab wounds, but only one wound was fatal.

Antistius had performed one of history's first recorded postmortem examinations, in which a physician looks at a body to find out how the person died. But forensics has always had limits. Although Antistius could point out the chest wound that had killed Caesar, he could not say who had struck the deadly blow.

Death in its many forms inspired the first forensic manuals. The oldest one was published in China in 1248. Called *Hsi duan yu* (The Washing Away of Wrongs), it tells how the bodies of people who have been strangled are different from the bodies of drowning victims. When a corpse is recovered from the water, says the manual, officers of the law should examine the tissues and small bones in the neck. Torn tissues and broken bones show that the victim met with foul play before being thrown into the water.

Poison was the subject of another landmark book in the history of forensics. In 1813 Mathieu Orfila, a professor of medical and forensic chemistry at the University of Paris, published *Traité des poisons* (A Treatise on Poisons). Orfila described the deadly effects of various mineral, vegetable, and animal substances. He laid the foundation of the modern science of **toxicology**, the branch of forensics that deals with poisons, drugs, and their effects on the human body.

As France's most famous expert on poisons, Orfila played a part in an 1840 criminal trial that received wide publicity. Marie LaFarge was accused of murder after her husband died. Orfila testified that he had examined the husband's corpse and found traces of arsenic.

▲ The deadly poison arsenic figured in many famous cases of poisoning. Today, however, poisoning more often involves toxic household substances or prescription overdoses.

LaFarge insisted that she had not fed the arsenic to her husband, and that he must have eaten it while away from home. The court, however, sentenced her to life imprisonment. Pardoned in 1850 after ten years in prison, LaFarge died the next year, claiming innocence to the end.

The LaFarge trial and similar cases highlighted the growing use of medical evidence in criminal investigations and trials. Courts were recognizing other kinds of forensic evidence, too. In 1784 a British murder case was decided by physical evidence. The torn edge of a piece of newspaper found in the pocket of a suspect named John Toms matched the torn edge of a ball of paper found in the wound of a man killed by a pistol shot. (At the time people used rolled pieces of cloth or paper, called wadding, to hold bullets firmly in gun barrels.) Fifty-one years later, an officer of Scotland Yard, Britain's famous police division, caught a murderer by using a flaw on the fatal bullet to trace the bullet to its maker. Such cases marked the birth of **ballistics**, the branch of forensics that deals with firearms.

Not all forensic developments involved murder. Science was also helping to solve crimes such as arson and forgery. By the early nineteenth century, chemists had developed the first tests to identify certain dyes used in ink. Experts could then determine the age and chemical makeup of the ink on documents, such as wills and valuable manuscripts, that were suspected of being fakes.

Forensics started to become a regular part of police work at the end of the nineteenth century, after an Austrian law professor named Hans Gross published a two-volume handbook on the subject in 1893. Gross's book, usually referred to as *Criminal Investigation*, brought together all the many techniques that scientists and law enforcers had developed for examining the physical evidence of crime—bloodstains, bullets, and more. Police departments started using *Criminal Investigation* to train officers. The book entered law school courses as well.

Modern forensic experts regard Hans Gross as the founder of their profession. Among other contributions, Gross invented the word "criminalistics." He used it to refer to the general study of crime or criminals. Today, however, the term has a narrower, more specific meaning. It refers to the study of physical evidence from crime scenes.

Almost every branch of science has been involved in criminal investigations. Meteorologists have testified about the weather on the date of a crime. Botanists have named the plants that produced tiny specks of pollen found on suspects' clothes. Dentists have matched bite marks on victims' bodies to the teeth of their killers. Anthropologists, scientists who study human beings, have helped police identify unknown corpses by supplying information about their gender, age, and ethnic background. Forensics is a vital part of modern crime solving, but it is part of historical research, too. Archaeologists, the scientists who study historic ruins, can use forensic techniques to examine ancient burial sites and battle-grounds as if they were crime scenes. Bullets fired long ago reveal their secrets to today's ballistics specialists. DNA tests solve historical mysteries that involve questions of identity. And to a forensics expert, even a thousand-year-old corpse has much to tell about how that person lived—and died.

The body of Napoleon Bonaparte, former emperor of France, was brought to Paris in 1840 and enclosed in this marble tomb in 1861. If the body holds secrets about Napoleon's death, they will not be revealed in the foreseeable future.

CHAPTER ONE

THE FATE OF
KINGS

▼ BEING A KING CAN BE DANGEROUS.

Throughout history, rivals have schemed to overthrow rulers and seize their power. Assassins have lurked in the shadows behind thrones. Revolutions have toppled mighty empires. Many royal deaths over the ages have been shrouded in mystery and uncertainty. Today forensic science is shining new light on some of these historical puzzles, including the fates of an Egyptian pharaoh, a French conqueror, and a Russian emperor and his family.

▶ THE SHORT LIFE OF TUTANKHAMEN

Today people call him King Tut, but 3,300 years ago he was the pharaoh Tutankhamen, ruler of Egypt. He became pharaoh as a child and was still a young man when he died after only ten years on the throne. Just as ancient Egyptian mummies are wrapped in cloth strips, Tutankhamen's life is wrapped in mystery. Egyptologists, the historians and archaeologists who study ancient Egypt, do not know for certain when this king was born or who his parents were. Some have suggested that Tutankhamen was a son of Amenhotep III, a powerful pharaoh who ruled Egypt during the first half of the fourteenth century BCE. Most experts, however, think that Tutankhamen was a son of Amenhotep's son Akhenaten, one of the most controversial pharaohs of all time.

When Akhenaten became pharaoh around 1352 BCE, Egypt was at the height of its wealth and influence. One of the kingdom's most powerful institutions was the priesthood of the god Amen. With large temples and vast estates under their control, the Amen priests not only governed Egypt's religious ceremonies, they shaped the country's economic and political life as well. Akhenaten, however, shifted the focus of worship to a different deity, Aten, represented by the sun. Eventually Akhenaten claimed that Aten was the only god, and that only he, the pharaoh, could speak to Aten on behalf of the people. Akhenaten moved the capital to a new city, Amarna, built and decorated in a new artistic style. He also had some of Amen's temples and monuments destroyed. Because the Amen priests resisted giving up their power, their property, or their beliefs, Akhenaten's reign was torn by social disorder and conflict between the priesthood and the pharaoh. After Akhenaten died, around 1335, Aten worship fell out of fashion, Amarna was abandoned, and the Amen priesthood regained its influence. Many of Akhenaten's new temples and monuments were destroyed, and his name was removed from wall carvings and lists of royal rulers.

Tutankhamen was born around 1342, midway through Akhenaten's reign, in a time of change and social conflict. As a child he was married to one of Akhenaten's daughters, who was probably his half sister (this was a way of keeping the royal bloodline in one family). When Akhenaten died, a royal prince named Smenkhkare became pharaoh. Smenkhkare may have been either Tutankhamen's brother or his uncle, but historians know little about him, and he ruled for just a couple of years. In 1333 Tutankhamen began his reign as pharaoh.

The young Tutankhamen had the guidance of several key advisers: Ay, the chief minister, who governed the country in the pharaoh's name; Horemheb, commander of the armies; and Maya, head of the treasury and one of Tutankhamen's personal attendants. The country's rulers worked to make Egypt stable and united once again. They rebuilt Amen's temples and restored the country's traditional art, religion, and social and political order.

At the age of eighteen or nineteen, Tutankhamen died. He may have fathered children, but none lived, so he left no heir. Ay became pharaoh, and then Horemheb took over. In later years the rulers of Egypt removed the names of Akhenaten, Tutankhamen, Smenkhkare, and Ay from monuments and records, erasing the so-called Amarna kings from history. That's why ancient Egyptian documents contain relatively little information about Tutankhamen's life or death.

Even the tombs of the Amarna kings were lost. Tutankhamen's tomb disappeared in the twelfth century BCE. It was buried beneath a thick layer of stone chips when another tomb was carved into the rock wall above it to hold the mummy of the pharaoh Ramses VI.

▶ A TINY TOMB AND A MESSY MUMMY

The discovery of Tutankhamen's tomb in 1922 dazzled the world. Although the tomb was broken into twice in

▲ A gold fan is one of many treasures recovered from
Tutankhamen's tomb. Despite the treasure, the tomb was
less splendid than those of most pharaohs.

ancient times, its inner rooms were never looted. They
were filled with astonishing works of art and beauti-
fully made household objects, placed in the tomb for
the dead king to use in the afterlife. But because some
things about the tomb were very odd, the discovery
also raised questions about Tutankhamen's death.

For one thing, Tut's burial place was unusually small and plain for a pharaoh's tomb. It appears that Tut was buried in an unfinished tomb, or one that was built for someone of a lower social class. This could have been done to conceal Tut's burial place, or because he was not highly honored by those who followed him in power. It is also possible that Tut was originally buried somewhere else, and that his mummy and grave goods were later moved into the tomb found in 1922.

Royal Egyptian burial chambers are decorated with wall paintings, but those in Tut's tomb are quite sloppy. Streaks and splashes of paint were never cleaned up. The work looks rushed and careless. Although the tomb contained many vases, statues, and pieces of furniture and jewelry covered with gold and gems, archaeologists have discovered that about 80 percent of these objects came from the tombs of other people. The first owners' names were removed from the articles and replaced by Tut's name. Even the sarcophagus—the large stone box that held the set of coffins containing the pharaoh's mummified body— was not made for Tutankhamen. Stoneworkers had chipped out the name of the original occupant.

The dead pharaoh's body was in an unusual condition, too. Normally, the mummification of a royal or noble body in ancient Egypt took about seventy days.

It was a careful process of removing internal organs, preserving the body with salts, plant resins, and other chemicals, and then wrapping the embalmed body in cloth. The usual result was a neat, dry package. Tutankhamen's mummy, though, had been placed in the inner coffin and then covered with large quantities of resin. It looked as though buckets of embalming resin had been poured over the mummy, creating a gummy mess that had later hardened like glue.

▶ HOW DID TUT DIE?

The unusual condition of Tutankhamen's tomb and mummy, together with the lack of written information about his death, made some archaeologists curious about how the pharaoh died. Tut appeared to have been embalmed and buried in haste—did that mean that there was something suspicious about his death?

Today when someone dies in suspicious or mysterious circumstances, a doctor called a **medical examiner** (**ME**) conducts an **autopsy**, an official examination of the body aimed at finding the cause of death. Autopsies are a vital first step in any forensic investigation. In the case of the long-dead Tutankhamen, the subject of the autopsy would be a 3,300-year-old mummy.

The first person to study Tut's mummy was Howard Carter, the British archaeologist who discovered the tomb. In 1925 he and a doctor named Douglas Derry

▲ Howard Carter (left), the British archaeologist who found Tutankhamen's tomb, carries artifacts from the burial chamber in 1922. Carter would later try to dissect the pharaoh's body.

examined the pharaoh's corpse. They had two big problems, though—they couldn't get the mummy out of the coffin, or the corpse out of the wrappings. Everything was stuck together with the old, dried resin. The men tried melting the resin in the sun, but nothing happened. Finally they simply hacked the mummy out of the mass of rock-hard glue and cut off the dried wrappings.

Carter and Derry discovered that Tutankhamen's body was less well preserved than most other ancient Egyptian mummified corpses. It was little more than a skeleton (and by the time they got it out of the coffin and the wrappings, it was in pieces). One theory is that Tut had died while he was on a hunting expedition, or while away from the capital for some other reason, which meant that his body was already decomposing when the embalmers started their work. Unable to preserve much of the king's flesh, the embalmers may have dumped extra embalming liquid on the mummy to cover the smell. Another possibility is that Tut's body was embalmed hastily or carelessly, and it was this idea that led some people to think the king had been murdered.

Carter and Derry's autopsy could not pinpoint the cause of Tutankhamen's death, although Derry did notice a small wound—possibly an insect bite or a scrape—on the dried, leathery left cheek of the corpse. Derry also noted that although the corpse's head had been shaved, it was covered by a waxy film. Such a film can appear on the body of a drowning victim, but it can also be caused by humidity, so it did not prove that Tut had drowned.

A different kind of examination of Tutankhamen's corpse took place in 1968, at the University of Liverpool in England. Professor R. G. Harrison made radiographs, or X-ray images, of the corpse from many angles. When Harrison studied the X-ray plates, he saw a fragment of broken bone inside the skull. He also saw a dark area in the skull, possibly caused by a blood clot or a blow to the back of the head. Harrison's findings made some people suspect that Tutankhamen was murdered, but there was no proof.

▶ WAS IT MURDER?

In the early twenty-first century, two Americans with backgrounds in law enforcement reviewed the case, hoping to determine whether Tutankhamen had been murdered. Michael King and Gregory Cooper focused on Tutankhamen's life, the people around him, and the possible motives those people might have had for wanting the pharaoh dead.

King and Cooper also met with a **forensic pathologist** (doctor who specializes in examining bodies), a radiologist (X-ray specialist), and a neurologist (doctor who specializes in the brain and nervous system). When these experts first looked at Harrison's 1968 X-ray evidence, they found a few surprises. There were tiny fractures, or breaks, in the small bones over Tutankhamen's eyes. Similar injuries happen when people fall backward. When the back of the head strikes the ground, the brain lurches forward, causing the fractures.

The experts also noticed that Tut's cervical vertebrae, or neck bones, seemed to be fused together. In other words, the vertebrae were locked into position as a single long bone, not a normal set of neck bones that move independently. The medical term for this condition is Klippel-Feil syndrome. People with Klippel-Feil cannot turn their heads. To look to the side, they must turn their entire bodies. They are also at high risk of injury from falls, because they cannot adjust their balance easily or protect their heads by holding them up.

In *Who Killed King Tut?*, King and Cooper argue that Tutankhamen probably died from a blow to the head or from a fall, perhaps after being pushed. They believe that the most likely murderer was Ay, the king's chief minister and adviser, who became pharaoh after Tut's death (and, according to some historians, married Tut's widow). Even if Tut's death was accidental, King and Cooper claimed that Ay was waiting for the chance to seize power and could have rushed the dead pharaoh into his unseemly tomb.

King and Cooper's view of Tutankhamen's death and Ay's wickedness made an exciting story, but it was based on circumstantial evidence—things that suggested that Tut's death was unusual but did not add up to solid proof. And by the time the medical experts finished their detailed review of the 1968 Tutankhamen X rays, they had decided that the images do not prove foul play, or even Klippel-Feil syndrome. In an article published in 2003, the experts point out that the bone slivers and fractures seen on the X-ray plates could have been created during the embalming process, or during the rough 1925 autopsy conducted by Carter and Derry. In addition, Tut's neck bones might have been perfectly normal. Resin lodged between the vertebrae may have made the bones look fused together on the X-rays.

In 2005 the Egyptian government allowed a research team to examine Tutankhamen's remains without

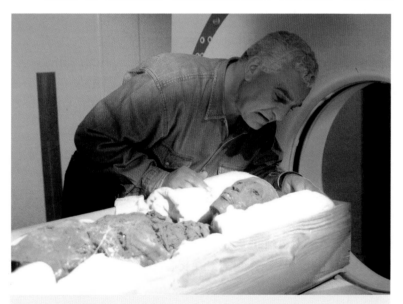

▲ Zahi Hawass, Egypt's leading archaeologist, prepares Tutankhamen's body for a computerized tomography (CT) scan in 2005.

further dissecting them, using medical technology known as computed tomography, or a CT scan. This scanning technique produced 1,700 three-dimensional color images of the king's body, inside and out. Zahi Hawass, chairman of the committee that governs the study of Egypt's ancient relics, reported that the scan showed no evidence of a blow to the head or any other sign of foul play. It did, however, show that Tutankhamen had broken a leg not long before his death. A research team suggested that the king may have died as a result of an infection to the leg.

No proof exists that Tutankhamen was murdered, or that he was not. Perhaps it is a question that forensic science will never be able to answer with absolute certainty. We know only that Tutankhamen died young and was buried with far less grandeur than was given to many other pharaohs who ruled ancient Egypt.

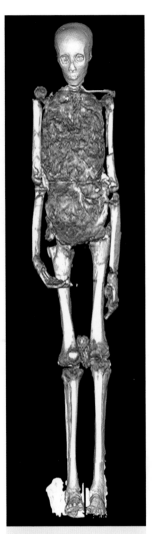

▲ More than 1,700 CT images of Tutankhamen's remains reveal no evidence of murder.

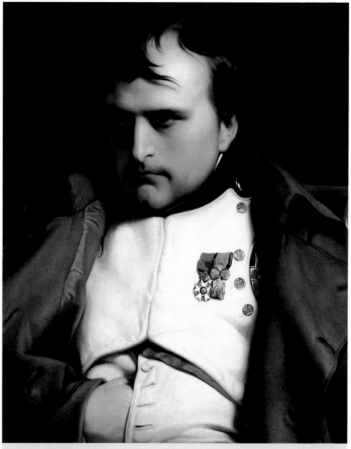

▲ French artist Paul Delaroche painted this portrait of Napoleon Bonaparte more than twenty years after Napoleon's death. The public remained fascinated with him.

▶ DEATH COMES FOR "BONEY"

Napoleon Bonaparte died on May 5, 1821, but it took a while for the news to reach the outside world. The former emperor had met his death on a remote island called Saint Helena, in the middle of the South Atlantic Ocean. Neither the telegraph nor the telephone existed. Sailing ships carried word of Napoleon's death to Europe, where people reacted to it in very different ways.

Until 1815, when the British defeated Napoleon in battle and sent him to Saint Helena, the people of Britain had lived in fear that he would invade their island as he had invaded and conquered many parts of Europe. As a result, the British felt no sadness at the death of "Boney," as they called him. Some cheered at the news. In France, however, many mourned the death of their onetime ruler, a general turned emperor who had made France a mighty power.

Some French people were suspicious about Napoleon's death, especially after the publication of their former emperor's will, in which Napoleon had written, "I am dying before my time, murdered by the English oligarchy [the group in power] and its hired assassins."

Most historians believe that Napoleon used the word "assassins" for the sake of drama. He was referring not to hired killers but to the British who guarded him. Troops marched outside his house day and night, disturbing his rest with the tramp of their boots, and infuriating him with the constant reminder that he

▲ After Napoleon escaped from a Mediterranean island, the British found a much more remote place of exile for him on the lonely, heavily guarded island of Saint Helena.

was their prisoner. Napoleon's archenemy, the British governor of the island, Sir Hudson Lowe, despised Napoleon. Lowe made no secret of the fact that he wanted the emperor's exile to be as miserable as possible.

Napoleon was idle and irritable on Saint Helena, and soon he became ill as well. He had trouble sleeping and suffered from headaches and pains in his joints. By 1817 he also had pain in his abdomen, as well as swollen legs and feet. Doctors could not agree on a diagnosis. Governor Lowe thought Napoleon was faking his symptoms in the hope of being returned to Europe.

By 1820 Napoleon was shaken by fevers, coughs, chills, digestive problems, and pain in various parts of his body. By March 1821 he could not leave his bed. Doctors turned to a technique called purging, in which a patient is given drugs to cause vomiting and diarrhea. Widely used in medicine at the time, purging was believed to cure sickness by removing as much as possible of the harmful contents of the stomach and intestines.

One of the doctors treating Napoleon gave him a medicine called tartar emetic. It brought on a spell of vomiting that left Napoleon weaker than ever. Another doctor, this one from the British navy, felt that the patient was in desperate shape. He administered a very large dose of a purgative called calomel. Napoleon vomited blood, fell into a coma, and died within two days.

▶ A BODY ON A BILLIARD TABLE

The day after Napoleon died, the governor ordered an autopsy to discover the cause of death. The autopsy took place on the billiard table of Napoleon's prison-home, Longwood House. At least eight doctors were present. Most were British, but one was from Napoleon's native island of Corsica. The Corsican doctor conducted the autopsy while the others watched.

No one was surprised to find that Napoleon's liver was enlarged. Most of the doctors who had treated him suspected some form of liver disease. There was no sign, however, that liver disease had killed him. The doctors saw a large ulcer in the stomach. They thought that it probably caused the bleeding during Napoleon's last hours. Finally, there was a swelling in the stomach. After much discussion, the doctors agreed that it was a cancerous tumor. Similar cancers had killed Napoleon's father and one sister. The verdict was that Napoleon, too, had died of cancer.

Rumors in France told a different story: Napoleon had been poisoned by the hated British. That rumor gained strength in 1840, when Napoleon's body was taken from Saint Helena to be reburied in France. The body was surprisingly well preserved—a phenomenon often seen in victims of arsenic poisoning.

▶ WAS NAPOLEON POISONED?

Arsenic in one form is a white powder with almost no taste or smell. It can easily be slipped into food or drink. Because the symptoms of arsenic poisoning look like those of many other illnesses, including food poisoning, it used to be hard for doctors and authorities to prove that arsenic had been used. For these reasons, arsenic was one of Europe's most commonly used poisons until 1836, when a British scientist named James Marsh developed an accurate chemical test that could detect even tiny quantities of arsenic. But the Marsh test was not used on Napoleon's body in 1840, and since the body was then entombed in a public monument in Paris, it was impossible for researchers to examine it.

Few historians took the idea of poisoning seriously. In 1950, however, a Swedish dentist and Napoleon fan named Sten Forshufvud read the diary of Napoleon's personal servant on Saint Helena. Forshufvud did not think that Napoleon could have died of cancer, because Napoleon was obese at the time of his death, while cancer patients are usually thin. The Swede believed that details in the servant's diary pointed to arsenic poisoning, and he set out to prove it.

With Napoleon's body out of reach, Forshufvud settled for the next best thing—he got hold of a lock of Napoleon's hair that one of Napoleon's servants had taken as a keepsake. Because hair absorbs arsenic from sweat and scalp oils, toxicologists—forensic scientists who specialize in the study of poisons and drugs—have learned to test hair when poisoning is suspected. In 1960 Forshufvud sent the hair sample to the Glasgow University Forensic Science Laboratory in Scotland for toxicological testing. Using a technique called neutron activation analysis (NAA), the scientists

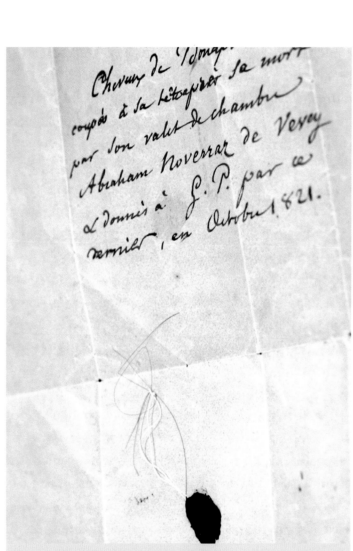

▲ A blob of wax holds several strands of hair that, according to the document, one of Napoleon's servants cut from the head of the dead emperor. The debate over Napoleon's death centers on souvenirs such as this one.

bombarded the hair sample with molecular particles called neutrons to make it radioactive. Because radioactive atoms of different chemical elements decay at different rates, analysts could determine the chemical makeup of the hair by measuring the rate of decay of atoms in the sample.

Arsenic is fairly common in the earth around us, and everyone's body and hair contain a small amount of it. The Glasgow lab, however, found that Napoleon's hair had 10 parts per million (ppm) of arsenic, compared with the normal level of less than 1 ppm. Another test, on a different lock of hair that had been kept by another of Napoleon's former servants, showed arsenic levels rising and falling along the length of the hair shaft—just what you would expect to find if a poisoner gave many doses of arsenic to his victim over time.

Together with several other amateur historians, Forshufvud developed a theory about who had poisoned Napoleon. Suspicion fell on Count Charles-Tristan de Montholon, one of Napoleon's associates who had accompanied him to Saint Helena. The investigators published several books about their poisoning theory in the late 1970s and early 1980s. In the most elaborate version of the theory, Montholon made Napoleon sick with doses of arsenic for years, then finished him off with another poison, perhaps cyanide, after he had been weakened by the medical purgings.

Later, forensic scientists examined the poisoning theory and the evidence for and against it. Some of these experts decided that the idea of murder by poison simply does not hold up. Two physicians, Philip Corso of the Yale University Medical School and Thomas Hindmarsh of Ottawa University, pointed out that according to the principles of forensic science, the presence of arsenic in hair is not enough to prove poisoning. The victim must also show some classic physical signs. The major symptoms of arsenic poisoning are spots of pigment on certain parts of the body, thick skin on the hands and feet, and bands of dark and white lines across the fingernails. The doctors present at Napoleon's autopsy wrote many descriptions of the body they had examined, but not one mentioned any of these symptoms. No doctor at the autopsy considered poison as a possible cause of death.

Since Forshufvud's first investigation in the mid-twentieth century, FBI forensic scientists and other researchers have found high levels of arsenic in other locks of Napoleon's hair (although one test, at the University of Toronto, found a very low level of arsenic). These results raise several points. First, it is impossible to know that all the souvenir locks were authentic. Even in exile, Napoleon was a major celebrity, and after his death untold pounds of other people's hair were in circulation as "Napoleon's hair." As early as 1861, one of Napoleon's former servants remarked that he had seen so many locks that were supposedly from the emperor's head that he could carpet the huge French palace of Versailles with them. Second, the original NAA tests in the 1960s were less reliable than modern tests, because the older equipment was less sophisticated and precise. The early results should be viewed with caution.

Still, the bulk of the evidence suggests that there is more than a trace of arsenic in Napoleon's hair. If that is true, how did it get there? And did arsenic kill him?

In the early nineteenth century, arsenic was an ingredient in many common products: medicines, makeup, wallpaper, powder for dusting wigs, and more. It was even used to preserve locks of hair as souvenirs or mementoes. So arsenic could have gotten into Napoleon's hair in a number of ways other than deliberate poisoning. As for Napoleon's death, arsenic poisoning cannot be ruled out, but Canadian physician Thomas Hindmarsh has a different idea. He thinks that Napoleon was accidentally killed by his medicine—specifically, by the big dose of calomel shortly before his death. This strong purgative could have made Napoleon's stomach bleed, bringing on an uncontrollable hemorrhage that was fatal to the former emperor.

▶ THE RUSSIAN ROYAL REMAINS

Russia was ruled by emperors called czars until 1917, when communist revolutionaries overthrew the imperial government, which had been in the hands of the Romanov royal family for more than three centuries. The communists imprisoned Czar Nicholas II, his wife, their son, Alexei, and their four daughters in a house in the Siberian mining town of Yekaterinberg.

In 1918 the seven Romanovs and four of their servants were herded into the basement of the house and

▲ Czar Nicholas II (second from left) posed with his children and nephews in 1917, the year he lost the throne of Russia.

executed on the orders of V. I. Lenin, the communist leader. Most were shot, but the bullets failed to kill several of the women. Jewels sewn inside the women's clothing for safekeeping had acted as body armor, and these survivors were stabbed and clubbed to death. The killers disfigured the bodies with sulfuric acid to make them unrecognizable, then buried them in a mass grave in the nearby woods. The great majority of historians have long accepted this version of the Romanovs' fate, which is based on statements by

▲ Assassins killed the czar and his family in this bloodstained basement room in the Siberian town of Yekaterinberg.

the executioners and by others who were in Yekaterinberg at the time.

After Russia's communist government fell in 1991, the new democratic leaders launched an investigation into the death of the Romanovs. A mass grave had been found at Yekaterinberg, and the remains it held were dug up and examined. There should have been eleven corpses, but the grave held only nine.

Ever since the execution, rumors about the children's fate had swirled through Russia and beyond. Some claimed that Crown Prince Alexei and his sister Anastasia had been killed and buried apart from the rest of the family, or had even escaped execution with the help of a sympathetic guard. The absence of two bodies from the grave suggested that two of the Romanov children had indeed met a separate fate.

Russian forensic scientists examined the Yekaterinberg bodies and invited a team of American experts to join them. The Americans were led by William R. Maples, a forensic anthropologist and specialist in identifying human remains. Based on the sizes and ages of the bodies, and on some very expensive dental work made of gold and platinum, Maples decided that the remains fit the descriptions of the czar, his wife, and three of their daughters. The bodies of one daughter and of the czar's son were missing.

The missing girl, Maples said, must be Anastasia, the youngest daughter, because the recovered female skeletons were older and taller than hers would have been. The Russians disagreed. After using computer imaging to compare the recovered skulls with photographs of the Romanov children, they decided that the missing daughter was Maria. Still, the fate of the czar and most of his family now seemed to be proved.

Further proof came in 1993, when Russian and British scientists analyzed DNA, or genetic material, from the remains. They focused on a part of the genetic signature called mitochondrial DNA, or mtDNA, which all children receive from their mothers. This type of DNA is inherited through the female line, remaining unchanged from generation to generation in a family. The mtDNA in bones can remain stable for a long time after death.

To test the Yekaterinberg samples, the analysts needed two things: a DNA sample from the body identified as that of Czarina Alexandra, wife of Czar Nicholas, and a second sample from someone who was known to be related to Alexandra through a female ancestor. Alexandra was the granddaughter of Queen Victoria, England's nineteenth-century monarch. Prince Philip, the husband of England's present monarch, Queen Elizabeth II, is Victoria's great-great-grandson. His mtDNA should match Alexandra's.

Philip provided a genetic sample to be used in the test. The lead analyst was Dr. Peter Gill of Britain's Forensic Science Service. He described the match between the two samples as "almost 99 percent." There is almost no chance, in other words, that the Yekaterinberg remains were *not* related to Philip, and if they were related, they had to be the remains of the Czarina Alexandra. Other tests showed that the body identified as Czar Nicholas shared mtDNA with several of Nicholas's living relatives, and that the youngest bodies in the grave were three daughters of Alexandra and Nicholas.

In 1998, on the eightieth anniversary of the executions, the Russian government placed the Yekaterinberg remains in the Romanov burial place in St. Petersburg, which had been the Romanov capital. Except for the missing two children, the fate of the Romanov remains was now known. Or was it?

▶ DNA DISPUTES

Not everyone was ready to agree that the bodies found at Yekaterinberg were the Romanov royal family. Both Russia's Orthodox Eastern Church and some of the surviving Romanov relatives have doubts about whether they should accept the findings of the forensic examinations and DNA tests. Perhaps they still hope that some members of the royal family met a kinder fate. Or maybe they fear that the modern Russian government cared more about closing a dark chapter of history than about making sure the remains were authentic.

Scientists have disputed the 1994 DNA tests, too. In 2004 Alec Knight of Stanford University, leader of a team of American researchers, made a startling announcement. He had compared Gill's report on Czarina Alexandra's DNA with genetic material from a preserved finger that was said to be that of Alexandra's sister, the Grand Duchess Elisabeth. (The finger had been removed from Elisabeth's coffin in 1982 and kept as a private relic by a bishop in New York.) According to Knight, Elisabeth's finger did not have the same mtDNA as Gill's sample from Yekaterinberg. The Yekaterinberg body could not be Elisabeth's sister.

The Forensic Science Service, where Gill had carried out his tests, agreed that the DNA from the finger did not match the Yekaterinberg body—but it added that the finger also failed to match Prince Philip's DNA. The finger, in other words, could not belong to the Grand Duchess Elisabeth or any other maternal relative of Alexandra.

Knight's team, however, also questioned the accuracy of Gill's 1994 tests, arguing that DNA-matching technology and standards were less reliable then than they are today. Knight thought that the DNA samples used in the tests could have been contaminated by people who handled the recovered remains. He also suspected that after more than seventy years in a shallow grave, the DNA in the bones would have been too badly degraded to provide the long, unbroken strings of genes that Gill claimed to have used in the tests at the Forensic Science Service.

Genetic researchers and forensic scientists from around the world have chimed in to support either Gill or Knight. Tom Parsons of the U.S. Armed Forces DNA Identification Laboratory, for example, argues that long DNA strings could easily have been preserved by the Siberian permafrost in which the bodies were found.

Unless the Yekaterinberg bodies are taken from their royal tomb and retested—which the Russian government is unlikely to permit—people will probably continue debating their identity. Nonetheless, many experts are satisfied that the bodies are those of the Romanovs. Meanwhile, the Romanov saga took a new turn in July 2007. Archaeologists working near Yekaterinberg found the remains of a bonfire and some bone fragments, teeth, bullets, and broken bottles that had

▲ Fragments of bone, glass, and bullets unearthed in 2007 near Yekaterinberg may solve the mystery of the two missing Romanov children.

once contained sulfuric acid. The human remains appear to be from a boy between ten and thirteen years old and a girl between eighteen and twenty-three. Alexei Romanov was thirteen when he disappeared. His sister Maria was nineteen.

Have the two missing Romanov children been found at last? The Russian government plans to test the DNA of the remains. As the earlier investigation shows, however, even high-tech tools such as **DNA testing** cannot always solve historical mysteries to everyone's satisfaction.

AFTER THE MASSACRE at Yekaterinberg, there were rumors that one or more of the czar's children was seen alive after the shootings. A few people surfaced in Europe, claiming to be either Anastasia or her brother Alexei. The best-known claimant was a German-speaking woman called Anna Anderson, who was sent to a mental hospital in Germany after trying to drown herself in a canal. Originally Anderson seemed to have amnesia, but in 1921 she claimed that she was the Grand Duchess Anastasia.

A number of people who had known Anastasia well, including some Romanov relatives, eventually met Anderson. Nearly all of them said that her claim to be Anastasia was a hoax, or perhaps a delusion caused by mental illness. A few Romanov relatives and friends, however, supported Anderson's claim. Two of her strongest supporters were the son and daughter of the Romanovs' doctor. Some researchers have suggested that these two organized the hoax or hoped to profit from it in some way. Meanwhile, a German nobleman hired a private detective to investigate Anderson's origins. The detective identified the woman as a missing factory worker named Franziska Schanzkowska. The factory worker's family, however, refused to get involved.

In 1938 Anderson filed a lawsuit in a German court to establish her identity as Anastasia Romanov and gain possession of an inheritance. By this time, her claim was known around the world. It even inspired a 1956 Hollywood movie, *Anastasia*, starring Ingrid Bergman. In real life, though, Anderson's story did not have a Hollywood ending.

The court case dragged on until 1970. Dozens of forensic experts on each side compared evidence, such as handwriting samples and the shapes of Anderson's and Anastasia's ears. In the end, the court ruled that Anderson had not proven her claim. She spent her final years in the United States, still claiming to be Anastasia.

Anderson died in 1984, and her body was cremated. A hospital where she had had surgery, however, had stored a sample of her tissue. In 1994 DNA from her tissue was compared with DNA from remains recovered at Yekaterinberg, and also with DNA from a known Romanov relative, Prince Philip of England. There was no match: Anna Anderson could not have been a Romanov. Her DNA was then compared to a sample from Franziska Schanzkowska's great-nephew. This time, it matched. The case of Anna Anderson was closed at last.

Graves mark the spots where soldiers fell at Little Bighorn Battlefield National Monument in Montana. Forensic research has shed new light on the historic battle that raged here.

CHAPTER TWO

SECRETS OF THE BATTLEFIELD

▼ ONE OF THE FASTEST-GROWING

fields in historical research is battlefield **archaeology**. Combining the careful digging methods of traditional archaeology with the techniques and tools that police use to investigate crime scenes, researchers are learning new things about old conflicts, such as the Battle of the Little Bighorn, also known as "Custer's Last Stand."

Some discoveries are rewriting history. The story of Spanish conquistador Francisco Pizarro's conquest of the Inca empire in Peru in the 1530s is familiar from history books, for example. But only recently have archaeologists, forensic scientists, and historians uncovered evidence of exactly *how* the Spanish won that fight.

▶ SHOWDOWN AT THE LITTLE BIGHORN

One of the first full-scale archaeological investigations of a battlefield took place at the Little Bighorn River in Montana, where American Indian warriors defeated Lieutenant Colonel George Armstrong Custer and some 210 U.S. soldiers in 1876.

The origins of the battle can be traced to the 1850s and 1860s, when the United States signed treaties that gave the Black Hills region, in what is now South Dakota, to the Cheyenne and Lakota Sioux people. Soon rumors spread that gold had been found in the Black Hills. In 1874 the U.S. government sent an expedition to investigate the rumors. Custer was its leader.

The rumors of gold were true. Soon hundreds of white miners swarmed into the Black Hills. This violated the treaties, but by 1876 the government had decided to ignore those agreements. It ordered the Indians onto reservations so that the newly desirable Black Hills country would be open to whites. The army sent troops into Montana, Wyoming, and the Dakotas to find the Indians and drive them to the reservations. Custer commanded a group of mounted soldiers called the Seventh Cavalry. It was part of a larger force, led by General Alfred Terry, that moved westward along the Yellowstone River toward the Little Bighorn River.

▲ George Armstrong Custer led U.S. troops into battle as part of an attempt to force American Indians onto reservations, in violation of treaties that the U.S. government had signed with them.

Terry sent the Seventh Cavalry ahead of the main force to scout the route. On the morning of June 25, Custer and his men reached a high point of land. Looking down at the valley of the Little Bighorn, they spied a large American Indian camp or village. It held as many as 7,000 people. Probably around a thousand of them were warriors. Custer had about 465 men.

Custer's next actions have sparked debate among military historians ever since. Instead of reporting back to Terry, he decided to attack. He sent 115 men off under Captain Frederick Benteen to prevent the Indians from escaping to the southwest. He then divided his remaining men into two forces: around 210 under his own command and 140 under Major Marcus Reno. The idea was that Reno would attack the south end of the camp and Custer would attack somewhere in the center, along the river, but it didn't work out that way.

When Reno launched his attack, the Indians fought back strongly. Reno lost more than thirty men. He and the survivors retreated to the top of a hill, where Benteen and his men soon joined them. The soldiers held out there, waiting for Custer (who had more soldiers than either Benteen or Reno) to come to their aid. Finally, on June 27, Terry's army arrived and the Indians retreated. A scout then rode up and reported tragic news: Custer and all his men were dead. Their bodies lay on a ridge above the Little Bighorn. Some had been mutilated and scalped, following American Indian war customs. They were eventually buried in a mass grave where Custer's body was found.

▲ Artist Feodor Fuchs based his Little Bighorn painting partly on information from Red Horse, a Sioux man who had fought there. American Indians are shown firing guns, a detail later confirmed by forensic work at the site.

▶ THE BATTLEFIELD AS A CRIME SCENE

News of the disastrous battle at the Little Bighorn reached the rest of the country as Americans prepared to celebrate the hundred-year anniversary of their country's independence. Early accounts of the battle presented Custer as a heroic leader who had fought bravely against overwhelming odds. None of his men survived to say otherwise, and few people were interested in American Indian stories about the battle. In 1890 marble markers were placed where Custer's men had fallen, and the battleground later became a national monument. In 1999 markers were put up for the thirty-two or so American Indians who died in the battle. By that time, our understanding of the battle had grown, thanks to a combination of nature and science.

Wildfires are all too common in the dry summers of the American West, and in August 1983 a fire swept across the Little Bighorn Battlefield National Monument. It cleared away the vegetation, letting archaeologists examine the ground more closely than ever before. Under the supervision of the National Park Service, archaeologists worked at the site until 1996. They collected more than five thousand artifacts, some of which are still being analyzed.

The researchers treated the battlefield like a crime scene. The first step was to search the site for every possible piece of evidence, especially cartridge cases and bullets. Volunteers who experience using metal detectors were enlisted for this part of the project. They marched in rows across the site. Whenever a metal detector showed something in the ground, the operator marked the spot with a small flag.

Recovery teams followed the detectors. They dug deep enough to locate the artifacts but left them in place. A third crew, the surveyors, followed the recovery teams. They measured and mapped the precise location and depth of every artifact before removing it from the ground.

Specialists in ballistics, the branch of forensic science that deals with firearms, examined the cartridge cases and bullets recovered from the battlefield. These experts were able to identify some bullets as having been fired from the same guns, which let them track the movement of individual weapons—and the soldiers who had fired them—across the battlefield. From this research, the archaeologists learned that after the fighting started, Custer's men split into several groups or wings, although it is not clear whether they did so on Custer's orders.

The trail of bullets also shows that when Custer began to retreat, he headed north to Greasy Grass Ridge (it has been renamed Last Stand Hill). If Custer had gone south, he and his men might have made it to the hill where Reno and Benteen were defending themselves. But as they fled north across a series of gullies and slopes, the Indians killed many of them. The survivors reached the slopes of Greasy Grass and scrambled toward the top, probably hoping to defend themselves there. However, the Sioux chief Sitting Bull had already led a group of American Indians up the hill from the other side. They came over the top and cut down Custer and the last of his men. Many of the bullets found at the battlefield came from single-shot Springfield rifles, the standard firearm of U.S. soldiers in 1876. The ballistics survey also showed that in addition to bows and arrows, the Indians had at least 415 guns, some of them undoubtedly taken from fallen soldiers. Among the nearly four dozen types of gun used by the American Indians at the Battle of the Little Bighorn were several models of Winchester and Henry repeating rifles. These were less accurate than the army's Springfields, but they could be refired much more quickly. Custer, the researchers concluded, was outgunned by his Indian opponents.

Human remains were another focus of the Little Bighorn archaeology project. The researchers dug around the marble markers that were supposed to mark the places where soldiers had fallen. Near most of them they found buttons, scraps of cloth, and finger or toe bones that had been overlooked when the skeletonized bodies were moved to the mass grave five years after the battle. There were also some skull fragments.

Forensic specialists who analyzed the bones said that they came from at least forty-four different men. Some of them had suffered what criminal investigators

▲ Sitting Bull, photographed six years after the Battle of the Little Bighorn, led the force that wiped out Custer and his remaining soldiers.

call blunt-instrument trauma—blows from heavy blunt objects. Black Elk, an Indian who was at the battle, later said that the warriors had killed some of the soldiers, or struck their corpses, with clubs and hatchets. In this case, the archaeological work at Little Bighorn confirmed an earlier report. The information about the soldiers' movements and the Indians' guns, however, were details about Custer's Last Stand that no one knew before the archaeological work at the battle site.

▶ AN INCA BURIAL GROUND

Historical discoveries can happen simply because someone digs a hole in the right spot. In 2004, in the capital city of Lima in the South American nation of Peru, the diggers were two archaeologists, Guillermo Cock and Elena Goycochea. The city was planning a new highway that would run across a suburban hillside called Puruchuco. The archaeologists thought there might be an old cemetery there. They dug a trench to find out—and found much more than they expected.

There was indeed a cemetery in the hillside, and it was very old. It contained the bodies of Incas, the people who ruled Peru before the Spanish conquest in the sixteenth century. The Incas traditionally buried their dead in a sitting position, facing east, and some of the Puruchuco bodies were arranged this way, in neat rows. Others, however, were lying face up or face down, pointing in all directions. These bodies did not have the traditional Inca funeral wrappings. They appeared to have been buried hastily, or under unusual

▲ Members of the archaeological team excavate one of the five-hundred-year-old Inca mummies found at Puruchuco.

circumstances. There were seventy bodies in all. Most were men, but a few were women.

When Cock, Goycochea, and their team started unwrapping the bodies, they saw signs of violent death—crushed skulls and broken bones. Two skulls in particular caught the archaeologists' attention. One belonged to a body they call Mochito, "the severed one." There were three holes in his skull. Each hole had four sharp edges, as though the skull had been pierced by a hard, four-sided, pointed object. Around one of the holes, the outer layer of bone was raised—the kind of damage that is caused when a weapon snags against bone as it is being pulled out of a skull.

Melissa Murphy, an anthropological archaeologist who examined Mochito's skull, determined that the holes in it probably had been made by a sharp-edged metal weapon. The Incas had no such weapons, however. They used stone clubs, stone-tipped spears, and slingshots.

Another skull had a round hole with clean edges, as though something had been driven through it with great force. Inside the skull was a plug of bone that fit the hole. The bones of the face were shattered. To the archaeologists, this injury looked like a gunshot wound in which the bullet had entered the skull and broken into several pieces, which tore apart the face on their way out. Francisco Pizarro and his men had metal swords, spears, and knives. They also had guns—early firearms called arquebuses. Cock, Goycochea, and Murphy suspected that they had made an extraordinary discovery at Puruchuco: the first bodies ever found of American Indians killed by the Spanish conquistadors.

▲ A gaping hole in the side of this skull is one of many signs that the Incas buried at Puruchuco died violent deaths.

▶ WOUNDS AND WEAPONS

The archaeological team needed scientific proof that the round head wound in one of the Puruchuco skulls was caused by a gunshot. They hoped that an X-ray image would reveal metal fragments around the edge of the wound, but they were disappointed. No metal showed up on the image.

Unable to shake the idea that the hole was a gunshot wound, the researchers thought that perhaps the metal fragments were too tiny for X-ray technology. They called in Tim Palmbach and Al Harper, forensic experts from a Connecticut crime lab. From their wide experience with gunshot wounds, Harper and Palmbach pointed out that a bullet from a modern gun would not punch out a plug of bone like the one found inside the Puruchuco skull. Instead, the force of the shot would break the bone into tiny bits. Sixteenth-century arquebuses, however, fired round balls of iron or lead. Such a ball could punch out a sizable plug of bone. The two experts noticed that the bone plug had a round depression on one side, like the print of a ball.

To examine the remains, Harper and Palmbach used a high-powered tool called a scanning electron microscope (SEM), which allows investigators to see things hundreds of times too small to be seen with the unaided eye. With this tool they found tiny particles of iron embedded in minute cracks in the bone all around the edges of the hole, and all over the surface of the bone plug. These particles strongly suggested that Cock and Goycochea were right: the skull belonged to an Inca killed by a sixteenth-century gun. He was the first known gunshot victim in the Americas.

Harper and Palmbach also examined Mochito and other bodies found in the Puruchuco mass grave. Along with the holes in his skull, which appear to have been made with metal weapons, Mochito had severe

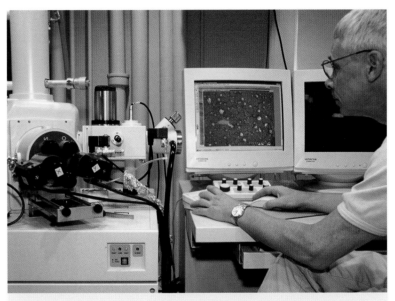

▲ A scanning electron microscope (SEM) allows researchers to see extremely tiny objects—such as particles of iron lodged in one of the Puruchuco skulls.

crushing injuries to his jaw and breastbone, as though rocks had fallen on him or a horse had trampled him.

Only three of the Puruchuco bodies show evidence of being killed by guns or metal weapons. The others show signs of blunt-instrument trauma. Their skulls had been shattered by blows with hard, rounded objects much larger than arquebus balls. When Harper and Palmbach viewed a museum display of ancient Inca weapons, they noticed heavy stone clubs that would have caused injuries like those on the Puruchuco skulls.

Were the Incas of Puruchuco killed by other Incas? To answer that question, the researchers would need the help of documents nearly five hundred years old.

▶ THE GREAT INCA REBELLION

The history of the Spanish conquest of Peru was written by the winning side. Modern historians know that some of the priests and chroniclers who wrote about the conquest wanted to play up Spanish courage and heroism. They presented the conquest as a series of dramatic battles, with a handful of conquistadors overcoming much larger Inca forces.

A different picture has emerged from the work of researchers who have combed through old Spanish documents *and* Indian histories. We now know that when the Spanish arrived, the Inca empire was falling apart, torn by civil war and uprisings. The Spanish took advantage of this unrest. They were able to conquer and hold Peru because they had help from Indian allies who had turned against the ruling Incas.

One of the central episodes of the Spanish conquest was the Great Inca Rebellion. The traditional conquistador histories tell that in 1536, four years after the Spanish took over, Incas across Peru united in an uprising against the foreigners. Pizarro and his followers were trapped in Lima, the new capital they had built. A huge Inca army besieged Lima, but the brave

Pizarro and his few hundred Spanish troops mounted their horses and hefted their weapons. In a mighty charge, they forced their way through the besieging army to the Inca leader, Quiso Yupanqui. They cut him down, and the rebels retreated.

Historian Maria Rostworowski has found documents stored for centuries in an archive in Spain that cast new light on the siege of Lima. According to one old report, Pizarro formed an alliance with a powerful Inca tribe in the mountains. One of the chief's daughters lived with Pizarro as his mistress in Lima. When Lima was besieged, she sent messengers to her mother, the chief. The mother sent an army to aid her daughter and her Spanish allies. Rostworowski thinks that the arrival of this army, not the Spanish charge, drove the rebel forces away from Lima.

Archaeologists Cock and Goycochea believe that the bodies buried at Puruchuco are those of Incas who rose against the Spanish in the Great Rebellion. They were killed by a combined force of Spanish conquistadors and their Inca allies (mostly by the Incas). Afterward, local people quickly buried the dead in a shallow ravine. Mochito's head was wrapped in a blue cloth, which may mean that he was the leader of the little band of rebels. From the nature of his injuries, he could have been killed by a Spanish cavalryman. Perhaps he died in face-to-face combat with Pizarro himself.

Despite his serene expression, Tollund Man did not die a peaceful death. He was hanged, probably by the cord that was found around his neck, then cast into a Danish bog some 2,500 years ago.

CHAPTER THREE

PUZZLES FROM THE PAST

▼ ROYAL ASSASSINATIONS AND WARS

are dramatic events, but historical research involves quieter mysteries, too. One long-lasting puzzle, for example, centers on a controversial map. Another concerns the so-called bog people, whose ancient but amazingly well-preserved bodies have been found across northern Europe. In both cases, forensic science has provided insights and information, although it has not settled every debate.

▶ THE VINLAND MAP

Today everyone knows that the Norse seafarers known as Vikings sailed from Europe to North America five hundred years before Columbus. Old Viking tales called sagas say that after the Norse established colonies on the large North Atlantic island of Greenland, they made voyages westward to a place they called Vinland. For years scholars suspected that Vinland was somewhere on the coast of North America, but they didn't know where.

In 1960 Norwegian researchers found the remains of a Viking outpost at L'Anse aux Meadows, a site on the island of Newfoundland, off the east coast of Canada. The site fits the sagas' descriptions of Vinland, and the ruins prove that Vikings visited the American coast around 1000 BCE. Even before the L'Anse aux Meadows site was discovered, however, a map seemed to offer proof of Vikings in America. If it is authentic, it is the oldest known map to show any part of the Americas, making it one of the most valuable documents in the world. But is it authentic?

The story of the Vinland Map begins in 1957, when an American rare-book dealer announced that he had bought a volume of medieval manuscripts from a European dealer. The volume consisted of two hand-copied books bound together, along with a map. The map showed Europe, Asia, and Africa. Unlike other medieval maps, however, it also showed part of the North American coastline, including an

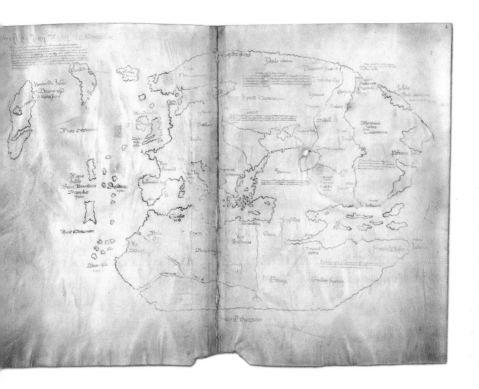

▲ Few documents have produced as much argument as the Vinland Map, which appears to show America years before Columbus's voyage. Is the map a rare relic or a clever forgery?

island labeled "Vinilanda." A document attached to the map was dated 1440, more than a half-century before Columbus arrived in the New World, as Europeans called the Americas.

The first experts to examine the map were from the British Museum. One of its manuscript analysts believed that although the handwriting of the two books looked authentically medieval, the writing on the map did not. In addition, the map had no provenance. In the business of buying and selling antiques, provenance is very important. Provenance is the record of who owned an object, or where it was located, up to the present. But although scholars have been studying medieval documents for hundreds of years, there was no mention anywhere of the Vinland Map before it turned up in 1957. The museum decided not to buy the map.

The map was next examined by experts at Yale University in New Haven, Connecticut. In 1965 Yale announced that the map was genuine, and a millionaire donor bought the map for the university. Archaeologists were digging and studying at L'Anse aux Meadows by that time, and the map and the site seemed to support each other.

Soon, however, other scholars and manuscript experts questioned whether the Vinland Map was authentic. Since the 1970s, Yale has made the map available for a variety of tests. Investigators have used some of the tools that are used by forensic specialists in cases of questioned documents, such as wills, checks, letters, or other papers that are suspected of being forgeries or frauds.

▶ REAL OR FAKE?

To test the age of the Vinland Map, forensic examiners have focused on the materials from which the map is made. It is drawn on parchment, a writing surface made from the skin of a sheep or goat. Because parchment is an organic material (something that came from an organism, or living thing), the Vinland Map can be tested with one of the most reliable tools in forensic science: **radiocarbon dating**.

All organic materials contain a form of radioactive carbon that decays at a steady rate after the death of the organism it came from. By measuring how much carbon has decayed, scientists can tell how much time has passed since the organism's death. Because radio-carbon dating destroys the sample that is tested, examiners had to use the smallest possible amount of material. They cut a thin strip three inches long from a blank space at the bottom of the map. A lab at the University of Arizona analyzed the strip. The results, announced in 2002, revealed that the parchment dates from around 1434, give or take eleven years.

The parchment is genuinely medieval, but what about the map drawn on it? A modern forger could

▲ Anatase crystals are the source of much debate about the Vinland Map. They are an ingredient in modern inks, but some researchers think they could occur in medieval inks as well.

have gotten hold of an old piece of parchment, perhaps a page from a book, then washed away its contents and drawn a map onto the blank surface. Such things have been known to happen. One of the books that was bound with the Vinland Map, in fact, seems to be missing some pages.

To determine the age of the map itself, experts have looked at two things: the ink used to draw the map, and the map's content—its drawings and words. The ink contains organic ingredients and could be radiocarbon dated, but the test would require a large sample—as much ink as the whole map contains. For this reason, radiocarbon dating cannot be used to determine the age of the ink on the Vinland Map. The ink has, however, been tested with other methods that use microscopically small samples.

The lines on the Vinland Map seem to have two layers: a yellow-brown pigment with a black pigment on top of it. Most of the black pigment has flaked off. This pattern is typical of iron-gall ink, one of several kinds of ink used in the Middle Ages. Iron-gall ink is made from lumps, or galls, that form on oak trees. It rusts over time, creating yellowish stains. As early as the 1970s, a chemist named Walter McCrone tested the Vinland Map ink and found very little iron in the yellow-brown lines. He did find large crystals of anatase, a form of the chemical titanium dioxide that was not used in ink until the 1920s. McCrone concluded that the map was a forgery. In the mid–1990s, some scientists challenged McCrone's analysis of the ink, but most experts who reviewed the case agreed that the ink seemed to be modern.

The ink dispute flared up again in 2003. Jacqueline Olin, a retired materials specialist from the Smithsonian Institution who had helped with the radiocarbon dating of the parchment, announced that she had made iron-gall ink using medieval methods and that it contained anatase. Yet the anatase crystals in modern inks—and on the Vinland Map—are larger than those from the ink Olin created. The map's anatase crystals have smooth edges, like modern manufactured anatase, while natural anatase crystals have jagged edges.

The black pigment on the Vinland Map shows evidence of carbon rather than iron. Soot-based ink, which contains carbon, was used in the Middle Ages, but it did not leave the yellow-brown stains typically caused by iron-gall ink. Some critics have suggested that a forger drew the map with yellow-brown ink, then overlaid the lines with traces of carbon-based black ink to fake the appearance of old iron-gall ink. Yet the map's yellow and black lines match perfectly except for one small spot on the British coast. Even some experts who consider the map to be a forgery think that it would have been extremely hard for a forger to trace the lines so well.

The Vinland Map's ink remains a problem. Many experts think that it is modern, but some well-qualified researchers argue that it could be medieval. What about the map's content? The experts disagree about that, too.

WHY FAKE A MAP?

IF THE VINLAND MAP is a forgery, who made it, and why? The usual reason for forging artworks or manuscripts is to sell them, but that does not seem to have been the case with the unknown creator of the Vinland Map.

The book dealer who sold the map to Yale did not have the skills to carry out such an elaborate hoax. Others, however, did possess those skills. In her 2004 book *Maps, Myths, and Men: The Story of the Vinland Map*, historian Kirsten A. Seaver reviews the evidence for and against the map and concludes that it is a modern forgery. Seaver thinks that the most likely creator of the map was Father Josef Fischer, a German priest who died in 1944. Fischer collected medieval manuscripts and was an expert on fifteenth-century maps. Seaver thinks that if Fischer forged the map, he probably did it as an intellectual game or joke, or to prove that he could pull it off, rather than for profit. Her case against him is backed by circumstantial evidence, but no proof.

Someday a letter or diary may come to light, revealing the origin of the Vinland Map and the reason why it was made. Until then, the mapmaker's identity remains an unsolved mystery.

· · · · ·

Some handwriting analysts think that the Vinland Map and the two books bound together with it are all the work of the same person. If so, the map could still be a forgery, but it would take a very dedicated hoaxer to forge so much material. Other experts—including a Yale paleographer, or specialist in ancient handwriting—have claimed that the map and the books were written by different people.

Those who question the authenticity of the Vinland Map point out that some of its language and information are out of place for the early fifteenth century. The map shows Greenland as an island, for example, although that geographic fact was not known until the late nineteenth century. No other medieval map that is considered genuine shows Greenland as an island. In addition, a few words or phrases on the map are more typical of Latin in the seventeenth century (or later) than in the fifteenth century. But while these points may suggest that the map is a fake, none of them proves it.

For now, the weight of the evidence indicates that the Vinland Map is a modern forgery on an old piece of parchment. Yet the case is far from closed. Arguments over the map will likely continue, unless some new forensic test settles the question beyond all doubt.

▶ BODIES FROM BOGS

A mummy is any long-dead body that is more than a skeleton. To be called a mummy, a body must have some soft tissue, such as skin, internal organs, or even eyes or hair. Mummies can be made in many ways. The ancient Egyptians mummified the bodies of their dead with chemical treatments, but mummies also form naturally when bodies are left in environments that prevent them from decaying. Ice, dry winds, and desert sands have turned corpses into dry mummies. Peat bogs preserve corpses, too.

A peat bog is an area of wet, spongy ground that is filled with peat, which is dense, fibrous vegetable matter that is slowly breaking down and turning into coal. Peat can be cut in blocks and burned as fuel. For centuries people have harvested peat in areas with many bogs in Ireland, Denmark, The Netherlands, and other parts of northwestern Europe. And for centuries people have found strange bodies in the bogs— shriveled, withered bodies with dark-brown flesh, sometimes wearing the remains of old-fashioned clothing such as skin capes.

In earlier eras, the bog bodies sometimes inspired fear and superstition. They seemed to be connected to earth spirits or dark magic. At other times, people thought the bodies were travelers who had fallen into

▲ A channel has been dug into this Irish peat bog. Blocks of peat, cut from the sides of the channel, are sold as fuel.

bogs and drowned. Some bodies recovered from bogs were reburied. Others were burned or destroyed in other ways. In the nineteenth century, however, peat cutters who found bog bodies started turning them over to local authorities or museums. The scientific study of the bog people had begun.

You might think that a wetland full of decaying plant life is the last place to preserve a body. Wouldn't a corpse decompose in such an environment? But most bogs are full of sphagnum moss, which contains a chemical called sphagnan. Scientists have discovered that sphagnan is a natural antibiotic, or killer of bacteria. In addition, bog water is high in acids and low in oxygen. Bacteria and fungi do not live in these conditions. Without bacteria and fungi, flesh does not rot. Instead, it hardens. Skin becomes leathery. Sphagnan also darkens the color of the skin, which is why most bog mummies are dark brown or brownish gray.

Even so, not all bog bodies are mummies. Fleshless skeletons or parts of skeletons—sometimes just skulls—have also been found in peat bogs. According to biologists who have studied peat bogs, conditions in the bogs are not uniform. Bogs change over time, and some bogs are less acidic than others, or have no sphagnan. In these bogs, flesh could decompose instead of becoming mummified.

▶ FORENSIC FINDINGS

More than a thousand bog bodies are known from northern Europe. Most are named for the places where they were found. One of the best-known bog people, for example, is called Tollund Man because he was unearthed from a peat bog near the Danish village of Tollund in 1950.

Scientists using carbon dating have been able to discover when the bog people died. The oldest known bog body is Koelbjerg Woman, who was no older than twenty-five when she died about ten thousand years ago. Unlike most bog people, she may simply have drowned.

Meenybraddan Woman was found in Ireland in 1978. She died just four or five hundred years ago, at the end of the medieval period, and was wrapped in a wool cloak before being buried in a peat bog. Perhaps she was a murderer or a suicide. Church law said that these people could not be buried in churchyards.

Most bog bodies date from the time that historians and archaeologists call the Iron Age, when people used tools made of iron. In northern Europe, the Iron Age lasted from about 700 BCE to 400 CE. Most of the bog people have something else in common. They died by violence.

Forensic scientists have examined the bog bodies as if they were modern crime victims. They have learned that bog people were killed in a variety of ways. Osterby Man, for example, died in the first century CE from a blow to the head. His head was cut from his body and thrown into a German bog. The head was found in 1948, with the hair still tied into an elaborate knotted hairstyle. Yde Girl, killed at the age of sixteen around two thousand years ago, was strangled and stabbed. Lindow Man died around the same time. He was hit on the head, then had his throat cut, and was finally strangled with a rope of animal tendons, which was found around his neck. Tollund Man's neck was encircled by a leather cord. He had been hanged, but his body was folded into a sleeping position before being put in the bog. Huldremose Woman died of knife wounds, hacked so savagely that her killers cut off one of her arms. Peat cutters found the arm near the rest of her body.

Why were the bog people murdered in such violent ways? The answer may lie in ancient Greek and Roman writings. The Greek historian Strabo, the Roman general Julius Caesar, and other writers reported that the tribes of northern Europe offered human sacrifices to their gods. The tribes also executed members of society who broke laws or codes of behavior. Modern scholars think that the bog bodies are probably the remains of people who were sacrificed or executed.

The bodies themselves may hold clues about the ancient killings. Yde Girl, for example, had a crippling deformity of the spine. Was she singled out for sacrifice because she was "unnatural"? The idea is only a guess, but it fits what anthropologists know about human sacrifice in some early cultures. Windeby Girl was about fourteen when she was killed, around 100 CE. Part of her hair was cut off, and her eyes were covered with a strip of wool. A man's body was found nearby. One theory is that the two were executed for having an improper relationship.

In another case that many people have speculated about, two bodies were found lying together in Bourtanger Moor in The Netherlands in 1904. One is a man. Another figure rests on his arms. When the bodies were discovered, people thought that the second figure was a woman, but it is now known to be another man. Is the position of the bodies an accident, or does it reveal a relationship between the two? If so, they could have been brothers or father and son. Another possibility is that they were lovers—homosexuality would most likely have been punished by death in that part of the world two thousand years ago. One of the men has a large chest wound. His intestines stick out through it. According to Strabo, some northern tribes believed they could read the future in the guts of sacrificial victims.

Grauballe Man, found in Denmark with his throat cut, has been studied in great detail. Like many other bog people, he died between 100 BCE and 100 CE.

Grauballe Man was so well preserved when his body surfaced in 1952 that scientists could analyze his stomach contents. His last meal was soup made of a fungus that causes hallucinations. Grauballe Man may have been in a fungus-caused trance during the ritual that ended his life.

▲ Grauballe Man, who lived at about the same time as the ancient Roman leader Julius Caesar, had his throat cut. His well-preserved remains included teeth, hair, and even fingerprints.

▶ TWO IRISH CORPSES

Lindow Man was discovered in England in 1984. For nearly twenty years afterward, no other bog bodies were found. Discoveries in the early twenty-first century, however, show that the peat bogs still hold surprises. In 2003 an Irish workman digging a ditch uncovered a headless, legless body. He called the local police. A detective viewed the remains and realized that he was looking at a murder victim—but the crime happened a long time ago. The remains, the torso and arms of a bog body, were turned over to the National Museum of Ireland. The Bog Bodies Project was formed, and a team of several dozen forensic experts began examining Oldcroghan Man, as he is called. Remarkably, they had a second bog body to study at the same time. Another partial corpse was found in 2003 at Clonycavan, 25 miles (40 kilometers) from the site of Oldcroghan Man. Clonycavan Man had his head, but his legs and hands were missing.

Radiocarbon dating revealed that Oldcroghan Man died between 262 and 175 BCE. Clonycavan Man died between 392 and 201 BCE. Forensic anthropologists agree that both men were in their early twenties when they died. Both were violently killed. Oldcroghan Man was stabbed and sliced, probably as torture. Holes were cut through his upper arms. The investigators found fragments of hazel wood in these holes. Sticks or ropes made of hazel switches may have been passed through these holes to hold the victim in place. Similar bindings have been found on other bog bodies. Oldcroghan Man was cut in pieces before being put in the bog. His head and legs have not been found. Clonycavan Man was also dismembered. First, though, he was killed by three axe blows to the head. The angle of the blows makes forensic experts think that Clonycavan Man was kneeling in front of his executioner.

The Oldcroghan and Clonycavan victims had certain things in common. They probably belonged to the upper classes of their societies. Both were well-nourished and in good health (up to the bloody end). Oldcroghan Man's hands are soft, with manicured nails and no sign of manual labor.

To determine a person's height from only part of the body, forensic scientists rely on **anthropometry**, the science of human measurements. A vast amount of information is available about the typical relationships between height, skull size, and arm and leg length. The Bog Bodies Project team used this anthropometric information to estimate how tall the two men were.

Oldcroghan Man was unusually tall: 6 feet, 6 inches (198 centimeters). Archaeologist Isabella Mulhall, organizer of the forensic team, says, "He's probably the tallest bog body known from Europe." Clonycavan Man stood 5 feet, 2 inches (157.5 centimeters) tall—a bit on the short side for people of his time and place. He made up for this, however, by piling his hair into a tall style held in place with a leather thong and a prehistoric version of hair gel. Chemical analysis revealed that his hair was coated with a mix of vegetable oil and resin from pine trees that grow only in southern France and Spain. The "gel" is evidence of trade across Iron Age Europe. It also says that Clonycavan Man, whoever he was, had access to what was probably a costly luxury product—and that, like people in every time and place, he cared about his appearance.

Who were Oldcroghan Man and Clonycavan Man? They lived well, by the standards of their societies. Were they chiefs or nobles who had the misfortune to be seized as prisoners of war, or executed by conquering enemies? Perhaps they were punished for betraying their communities, or carefully groomed for sacrifice. Although forensic science has told us much about the bog bodies, the reasons for the long-ago deaths remain unknown.

▶ UNANSWERED QUESTIONS

Forensic science can tell us how and when the bog people died, but we may never know why. The best historians and archaeologists can do is offer educated guesses—and that is true of much historical research. History has plenty of unanswered questions. What happened on Roanoke Island, off the coast of North Carolina, where colonists started a settlement in the 1580s, then disappeared? Who was Jack the Ripper, the savage killer who stalked the streets of London in 1888 and taunted the police with mocking letters? People have studied these questions for years but have found no definite answers.

In science fiction stories, people solve historical mysteries by going back to the past in time machines. Without such technological miracles, historical researchers must rely on other means of investigating the past. One of their most useful tools is forensic science. As new forensic techniques are developed in the future, investigators will use them not just to solve new crimes but to explore the mysteries of the past.

▼ GLOSSARY

anthropometry the science of human measurements; used to estimate overall body size when only part of a body is available for study

archaeology the study of ancient people and cultures through examination of ruins and other physical traces

autopsy a medical examination performed on a body to find the cause of death; a forensic autopsy also tries to establish the time of death, and whether the death was natural, accidental, suicide, or homicide

ballistics the branch of forensic science that deals with guns, gunshot patterns, and bullets

DNA deoxyribonucleic acid, which contains each individual's genetic code and is found in tissue, saliva, and other cells

DNA testing the use of DNA to identify individuals; DNA testing may match a person to a piece of evidence or establish a blood relationship between two people

forensic pathologist physician who specializes in examining the dead and identifying the causes of death and disease

forensic science the use of scientific knowledge or methods to investigate crimes, identify suspects, and try criminal cases in court

forensics in general, debate or review of any question of fact relating to the law; often used to refer to forensic science

medical examiner public official responsible for determining cause of death (sometimes called coroner)

postmortem after death; postmortem injuries to a body, for example, occur after the person has died

radiocarbon dating a process that measures the amounts of a form of radioactive carbon that starts to decay when an organism dies; by measuring how much carbon has decayed in a sample of bone, wood, leather, or other organic material, scientists can estimate how long ago the specimen was alive; used in archaeology and forensics

toxicology the branch of medical and forensic science that deals with drugs, poisons, and harmful substances

▼ FIND OUT MORE

FURTHER READING

Campbell, Andrea. *Forensic Science: Evidence, Clues, and Investigation*. Philadelphia: Chelsea House, 2000.

Friedlander, Mark Jr., and Terry Phillips. *When Objects Talk: Solving a Crime with Science*. Minneapolis, MN: Lerner, 2001.

Funkhluser, John. *Forensic Science for High School Students*. Dubuque, IA: Kendall Hunt, 2005.

Mattern, Joanne. *Forensics*. San Diego, CA: Blackbirch Press, 2004.

Owen, David. *Police Lab: How Forensic Science Tracks Down and Convicts Criminals*. Toronto: Firefly, 2002.

Platt, Richard. *Crime Scene: The Ultimate Guide to Forensic Science*. New York: Dorling Kindersley, 2003.

Yeatts, Tabatha. *Forensics: Solving the Crime*. Minneapolis, MN: Oliver, 2001.

WEB SITES

www.aafs.org/yfsf/index.htm

The Web site of the American Academy of Forensic Sciences features the Young Forensic Scientists Forum, with information on careers in forensics. The site also has links to other Internet resources.

www.archaeology.org/online/features/bog/

The Bodies of the Bogs, a site maintained by the Archaeological Institute of America, offers an introduction to the study of Europe's bog people.

www.bbc.co.uk/history/archaeology/excavations_techniques/ two_men_01.shtml
This article on the Web site of the British Broadcasting Corporation is a good introduction to battlefield archaeology.

www.courttv.com/forensics_curriculum/
Developed by CourtTV (now truTV), the American Academy of Forensic Sciences, and the National Science Teachers Association, this kid-friendly Forensics in the Classroom site introduces forensic science with a glossary, time line, and virtual forensics lab.

www.forensicmag.com/
Forensic Magazine's Web page features case studies and news about developments in criminalistics and other branches of forensic science.

www.pbs.org/wgbh/nova/inca/
The Public Broadcasting System (PBS) site about the Great Inca Rebellion describes the forensic techniques that scientists used when examining ancient remains found in mass graves in Peru.

www.pbs.org/wgbh/nova/vinland/
A companion to a PBS *NOVA* show, this Web page presents an overview of the evidence for and against the Vinland Map.

▼ BIBLIOGRAPHY

The author found these books and articles especially helpful when researching this volume.

Bell, Suzanne. *Encyclopedia of Forensic Science.* New York: Facts On File, 2004.

Boyer, Richard S., Ernst A. Rodin, Todd C. Grey, and R. C. Connolly, "The Skull and Cervical Spine Radiographs of Tutankhamen: A Critical Appraisal," *American Journal of Neuroradiology,* 24 (June/July 2003), pp. 1142–1147. Reproduced in King and Cooper, *Who Killed King Tut?*

Choi, Charles. "Drawing the Lines: Is a Pre-Columbus Map of North America Truly a Hoax?" ScientificAmerican.com, March 1, 2004, online at http://www.sciam.com/article.cfm?chanID=sa004&articleID=00069D8F-B5FC-101E-B40D83414B7F0000

Evans, Colin. *The Father of Forensics: The Goundbreaking Cases of Sir Bernard Spilsbury and the Beginnings of Modern CSI.* New York: Berkley, 2006.

———. *A Question of Evidence: The Casebook of Great Forensic Controversies, from Napoleon to O.J.* Hoboken, NJ: John Wiley & Sons, 2003.

King, Michael R., and Gregory M. Cooper. *Who Killed King Tut? Using Modern Forensics to Solve a 3,300-Year-Old Mystery.* Amherst, NY: Prometheus Books, 2004.

MacQuarrie, Kim. *The Last Days of the Incas.* New York: Simon & Schuster, 2007.

Maples, William R. *Dead Men Do Tell Tales: The Strange and Fascinating Cases of a Forensic Anthropologist.* New York: Doubleday, 1994.

Pollard, Tony, and Neil Oliver. *Two Men in a Trench: Battlefield Archaeology—The Key to Unlocking the Past.* London: Michael Joseph, 2002.

Ramsland, Katherine. *The C.S.I. Effect.* New York: Berkley, 2006.

Saferstein, Richard. *Criminalistics: An Introduction to Forensic Science.* Upper Saddle River, NJ: Prentice Hall, 2003.

Seaver, Kirsten A. *Maps, Myths, and Men: The Story of the Vinland Map.* Palo Alto, CA: Stanford University Press, 2004.

Wecht, Cyril, and Greg Saitz. *Mortal Evidence: The Forensics Behind Nine Shocking Cases.* Amherst, NY: Prometheus, 2003.

▼ INDEX

▼ ABOUT THE AUTHOR

REBECCA STEFOFF has written many books on scientific subjects for young readers. She has explored the world of evolutionary biology in Marshall Cavendish's Family Trees series; she also wrote *Microscopes and Telescopes* and *The Camera* for the same publisher's Great Inventions series. After publishing *Charles Darwin and the Evolution Revolution* (Oxford University Press, 1996), Stefoff appeared in the *A&E Biography* program on Darwin and his work. She lives in Portland, Oregon. You can learn more about her books for young readers at **www.rebeccastefoff.com**.